SECRET ORIGIN

Geoff Johns
Writer

Ivan Reis
Penciller

Oclair Albert
Inker

Randy Mayor
Colorist

Rob Leigh
Letterer

With
Julio Ferreira Partial Inker Book 3
Ivan Reis Partial Inker Book 6

Cover by **Ivan Reis** and **Oclair Albert**

Original Series Covers by
Ivan Reis and **Dave McCaig**

Eddie Berganza Editor-original series
Adam Schlagman Associate Editor-original series
Bob Harras Group Editor-Collected Editions
Sean Mackiewicz Editor
Robbin Brosterman Design Director-Books

DC COMICS
Diane Nelson President
Dan DiDio and Jim Lee Co-Publishers
Geoff Johns Chief Creative Officer
Patrick Caldon EVP-Finance and Administration
John Rood EVP-Sales, Marketing and
            Business Development
Amy Genkins SVP-Business and Legal Affairs
Steve Rotterdam SVP-Sales and Marketing
John Cunningham VP-Marketing
Terri Cunningham VP-Managing Editor
Alison Gill VP-Manufacturing
David Hyde VP-Publicity
Sue Pohja VP-Book Trade Sales
Alysse Soll VP-Advertising and Custom Publishing
Bob Wayne VP-Sales
Mark Chiarello Art Director

**GREEN LANTERN: SECRET ORIGIN
(NEW EDITION)**

Published by DC Comics. Cover, text and compilation
Copyright © 2010 DC Comics. All Rights Reserved.

Originally published in single magazine form in
GREEN LANTERN 29-35. Copyright © 2008
DC Comics. All Rights Reserved. All characters, their
distinctive likenesses and related elements featured
in this publication are trademarks of DC Comics.
The stories, characters and incidents featured in this
publication are entirely fictional. DC Comics does not
read or accept unsolicited submissions of ideas,
stories or artwork.

DC Comics, 1700 Broadway, New York, NY 10019
A Warner Bros. Entertainment Company
Printed by Quad/Graphics, Versailles, KY, USA.
10/27/10. First printing.

ISBN: 978-1-4012-3085-2

SUSTAINABLE
FORESTRY
INITIATIVE
Certified Chain of Custody
Promoting Sustainable
Forest Management
www.sfiprogram.org
Fiber used in this product line meets the
sourcing requirements of the SFI program.
www.sfiprogram.org PWC-SFICOC-260

INTRODUCTION BY **RYAN REYNOLDS**

I was never an expert on Hal Jordan. I'd always known the basic gist of the character: I knew he wore a lot of green. Had a ring possessed of infinite power bestowed upon him by a dying alien. And I knew he's survived many successors and wildly diverse iterations over an astonishing multi-decade run. If you like sports analogies, he's the New York Yankees. Lately though, I've gotten to know the guy pretty damn well. Like Hal Jordan, I too was given the gift of a ring. Mine was more symbolic in its power but no less auspicious. I was asked to put that ring on and bring Hal Jordan to life in a whole new form: Film. Not a job I take lightly.

About a year and a half ago, I first sat down with Martin Campbell, Donald DeLine, and a man whom I consider responsible for the resurgent interest in Green Lantern, Geoff Johns. They were all eager to build a big screen superhero who would both live up to his lengthy legacy, yet simultaneously find a foothold with a whole new audience – young and old alike. Hal Jordan was about to become a living, breathing person. And I was going to be the guy to do it. No pressure...

True fans of Hal Jordan know the caliber of hero we're talking about. From the moment I came aboard, I saw the challenge and opportunity in creating a classic yet modern day hero who can throw a punch, tell a joke and kiss the girl. I saw the guy as a cross between Chuck Yeager and Han Solo. The Green Lantern saga is so limitless in its scope, I'm sure it was a relief for the writers to know it was going to be an origin story of sorts. They need look no further than the starting point.

Green Lantern encompasses a seemingly limitless supply of adventure: fighter jets, space travel, action, aliens, betrayal, humor, tragedy, heroes, villains, and even a rather complicated little love story. These are just a few ingredients which have been a part of this epic for over 50 years.

It's a great time to be a superhero fan. Technology is such that bringing Green Lantern to life properly is finally possible. Creating energy constructs based upon infinite will and pure imagination can vividly appear before our very eyes. This technological leap also happened to coincide with a time period in which the world is fascinated by big screen comic book adaptations.

Preparing to get Hal up and running in living color was helped greatly by this book, SECRET ORIGIN, illustrated beautifully by Ivan Reis who I had the pleasure of meeting on the set in New Orleans. This book basically gave me the introduction I was looking for in order to begin the incredible ascent to Oa. I hope you like it.

Actor **Ryan Reynolds** stars as Hal Jordan in the upcoming Green Lantern movie.

"WHAT ARE YOU AFRAID OF?"

PEOPLE LIKE TO ASK ME THAT. WHEN THEY DO, THEY HAVE THIS KNOWING GRIN ON THEIR FACES. AS IF THEY EXPECT ME TO ANSWER, "NOTHING."

I HUMOR THEM MOST OF THE TIME, BECAUSE THAT'S WHAT THEY WANT ME TO SAY.

"I'M NOT AFRAID OF ANYTHING."

THEY THINK I WAS BORN WITHOUT FEAR.

THEY'RE WRONG.

THEY THINK THIS RING GIVES ME THE POWER TO DO ANYTHING.

THEY'RE WRONG ABOUT THAT TOO.

BEFORE I WAS GIVEN THE GREATEST WEAPON IN THE UNIVERSE, BEFORE I JOURNEYED TO THE STARS--

--MY DAD GAVE ME THE POWER TO DO ANYTHING.

HE TOLD ME I COULD BE WHATEVER I WANTED TO BE.

DAMMIT. I'M HAVING SOME **PROBLEMS** HERE, FERRIS. OIL'S GETTIN' EATEN UP **QUICK.** I THINK THE LAST OF MY TORQUE PINS JUST FAILED.

I THOUGHT THIS WAS SENT TO I-LEVEL REPAIR.

IT **WAS.**

DADDY!

DADDY, THAT BOY IS BREAKING THE **RULES!**

ONE MINUTE, HONEY, OKAY?

I NEED TO BRING IT IN. AWAY FROM THE CROWD.

THERE'S NO EXTERNAL LEAKAGE. THE INVESTORS ARE **WATCHING.**

THAT'S **FIFTEEN-MILLION DOLLARS** AND OUR LAST **SIX YEARS** OF **DEVELOPMENT** YOU HAVE IN THE **AIR.**

KEEP IT **FLYING,** JORDAN.

THIS THING'S GOING **DOWN,** FERRIS.

ON TOP OF YOU, COAST CITY, OR RIGHT HERE...

...AND **RIGHT HERE** NO ONE ELSE GETS HURT.

WHEN YOUR WORST FEAR HAPPENS IN FRONT OF YOUR EYES--

DAD.

--I THOUGHT THERE WAS NOTHING **LEFT** TO BE AFRAID OF.

MOM THOUGHT THERE WAS EVERYTHING.

YAHOO!

KEN ARDEN FLEW IN THE AIR FORCE WITH DAD AND CARL FERRIS. AFTER DAD DIED, ARDEN STARTED HIS OWN AEROSPACE TESTING FACILITY.

THAT WAS PERFECT FOR ME. I SWORE TO MOM THAT I'D NEVER GO TO FERRIS AIR AGAIN--

--BUT I CAUGHT THE BUS TO ARDEN AVIATION EVERY CHANCE I GOT. THERE WAS A BROKEN LOCK ON THE SOUTH GATE THAT THEY DIDN'T USE ANYMORE. IT WAS EASY ENOUGH TO GET IN.

EASY ENOUGH TO CLIMB THE LADDER UP TO THE TOP OF HANGAR 3, TOO.

THERE WASN'T A BETTER VIEW IN THE WORLD.

YEAH!

HAL?!

HAL, HOW IN THE *WORLD* DID YOU--?

I JUMPED.

DON'T WORRY, MR. ARDEN, I CAN GET DOWN MYSELF. IT'S LIKE A GIANT FIREMAN'S POLE!

DON'T YOU MOVE!

I'M SO *SORRY,* KEN.

IT'S OKAY, JESSICA...

...HE'S JUST GOT A LOT OF HIS FATHER IN HIM.

HOW MANY *TIMES* HAVE YOU *PROMISED* ME YOU WOULDN'T GO TO THE AIRFIELDS, HAL?

YOU SAID *FERRIS AIR.*

YOU ARE NOT ALLOWED *ANYWHERE* NEAR A PLANE, DO YOU UNDERSTAND ME, YOUNG MAN?

DO YOU?

YES, MA'AM.

I DIDN'T *UNDERSTAND* HER.

AND SHE DIDN'T *UNDERSTAND* ME.

NO ONE DID.

NICE GOING, *JERK.*

SHUT *UP,* JACK.

MOM WAS *FREAKING OUT* WHEN MR. ARDEN CALLED. SHE ALMOST HAD A HEART ATTACK!

OW.

YOU SCARE MOM LIKE THAT AGAIN AND THERE'S PLENTY MORE.

DON'T FIGHT! DON'T FIGHT!

WE'RE *NOT,* JIM.

WE AREN'T MOVING.

BUCKLE UP.

BETTER SAFE THAN SORRY. MOM SAYS SO.

BUCKLE UP.

BEFORE MOM HAS TO TELL YOU TO.

KLIK

SON?

CAN I HELP YOU?

I'M EIGHTEEN TODAY, SIR.

BOOOMM

MAJOR JONATHAN "HERC" STONE. HE FLEW WITH MY FATHER, CARL FERRIS AND KEN ARDEN. THEY WERE KNOWN AS THE *FOUR MUSKETEERS.*

STONE WAS THE ONLY ONE WHO CONTINUED HIS CAREER IN THE USAF. HE EARNED SO MANY SILVER STARS HE OUTNUMBERED THE AMERICAN FLAG.

HE DIDN'T LIKE ME VERY MUCH.

HE'S APPROACHING *MACH THREE,* MAJOR.

MACH *THREE?!*

MACH *THREE.*

THREE POINT ONE.

HAHA *HAAA!* I'VE GOT HER *REALLY* KICKING NOW!

DAMMIT, HIGHBALL, WE'RE TESTING STRUCTURAL LIMITATIONS AT MACH *ONE,* SHE'S NOT READY TO--

GIVE HER SOME *CREDIT,* MAJOR! SHE'S STILL HOLDING AT MACH THREE POINT *TWO!*

MACH THREE POINT *THR--!*

RRRRRMMMMBBBBLLL

TING TING TING

HEY, STONE...

COAST CITY WAS LESS THAN HALF AN HOUR FROM EDWARDS. TWENTY MINUTES FROM FORT ROCK.

AND THERE WAS ALWAYS A BATTLESHIP OR THREE IN THE HARBOR.

COAST CITY WAS A MILITARY TOWN.

AND FRIDAY NIGHT, IT ALWAYS LIT UP LIKE A ROCKET. THAT NIGHT, IT WAS PACKED BY THE AIR FORCE AND THE MARINES, READY FOR TAKE OFF.

...YOU'RE THE *BEST SHOT* IN THE CORPS, WE'D *HATE* TO LOSE YOU.

...YOU'RE *SCREWED*, HIGHBALL. YOU PISSED OFF STONE. YOU *INVALIDATED* HIS ENTIRE *TWO-YEAR* PROGRAM.

I SAVED THE AIR FORCE *TWO YEARS* OF TEST FLIGHTS. THE F-16'S READY FOR COMBAT *NOW*, ROCKET-MAN.

YOU *DESTROYED* A THIRTY MILLION DOLLAR *JET* TO PROVE THAT?

IF THAT'S WHAT IT TAKES TO GET OUR PILOTS IN THE *SAFEST* EQUIPMENT *SOONER* THAN *LATER*, FINE.

STONE'S GONNA TAKE THIS OUT ON *ALL* OF US.

THAT'S WHY THE *DRINKS* ARE ON *ME*.

LET *GO*.

YOU'RE COMING *HOME* WITH *ME*, CINDY.

NO, I'M *NOT*.

I'M NOT GOING *ANYWHERE*!

YOU'RE COMING NOW OR I'LL *SNAP* YOUR NECK.

HEY, WARTHOG. THE LADY DOESN'T WANT TO GO WITH YOU.

MIND YOUR OWN BUSINESS, FLYBOY.

THAT HURTS--

--OWW!

KRRAKK

YOU SEE THAT, STEWART?

THAT *JET JOCKEY* JUST KNOCKED DOWN ONE OF *OURS*.

HERE WE GO.

HERE WE GO.

HEN IT COMES TO WAR, WE MIGHT ALL BE ON HE SAME SIDE. BUT IF YOU THINK THERE'S NO TERSERVICE RIVALRY BETWEEN THE MERICAN ARMED FORCES--

--YOU'RE AS SHARP AS A *JARHEAD*.

YOU SHOULD BE *HAPPY*.

THIS IS MORE *FIGHTING* THAN THE AIR FORCE WILL SHOW YOU ALL YEAR.

THEN I BETTER MAKE IT *COUNT*.

HAL?

JIM?

IT'S PAST *TWO* IN THE MORNING. WHAT ARE YOU DOING--?

I KNOW THIS IS YOUR HANGOUT. I'VE BEEN WAITING FOR YOU. LIKE ALWAYS.

BRO, I--

MOM'S DYING.

WHAT IS IT?

CANCER. IT STARTED IN THE PANCREAS. AND IT'S *BAD.*

I NEED TO SEE HER.

YOU *CAN'T.*

WHAT DO YOU MEAN I CAN'T?

YOU KNOW WHAT MOM SAID. AS LONG AS YOU'RE IN THE AIR FORCE--

THIS IS *DIFFERENT,* JIM.

THE DOCTORS SAID THE STATE SHE'S IN, ANYTHING *UPSETTING* COULD TRIGGER ALL SORTS OF *PHYSICAL* PROBLEMS.

JACK WON'T LET YOU.

I CAN'T LET YOU EITHER.

THE NEXT MORNING, I GOT TO BASE EARLY. INSTEAD OF REPORTING RIGHT TO STONE'S OFFICE, I TOOK AN UNAUTHORIZED JOYRIDE.

IT WAS THE FIRST TIME I DIDN'T SMILE IN THE AIR.

WHEN I LANDED, STONE WAS WAITING FOR ME.

...THE LAST TIME THE AIR FORCE LOST THIS MANY JETS IN *ONE WEEK* WE WERE AT WAR IN VIETNAM.

NOW I'VE GOT TO CALL THE PENTAGON AND EXPLAIN HOW WE LOST A THIRTY MILLION DOLLAR FIGHTER ON A DAMN *TEST FLIGHT* TO DETERMINE...

..."STRUCTURAL LIMITATIONS OF THE F-16 AT MACH ONE." THIS WASN'T EVEN A *COMBAT* SIMULATION!

YOU MAY BE THE "*BEST*" PILOT ON *PAPER*, BUT IN *REALITY* YOU'RE THE MOST *EXPENSIVE* AND THE *MOST DANGEROUS*.

IT'S TIME YOU USE THAT *LUMP* ON YOUR SHOULDERS ONCE IN AWHILE.

STONE'S WORDS WERE JUST A FOG AROUND ME. LIKE JACK'S.

BUT I ALWAYS LISTENED TO JIM. AND THAT'S ALL I WAS HEARING.

"MOM'S DYING."

I JUST TOOK HER FOR A SPIN, MAJOR.

WITHOUT CLEARANCE AND WITHOUT AUTHORIZATION, JOYRIDING LIKE IT WAS YOUR *LAST* FLIGHT.

IT WAS. I KNEW IT WAS.

I COULDN'T SAY IT, I COULDN'T WALK AWAY, I COULDN'T QUIT.

I HAD TO FIND ANOTHER WAY OUT.

ANOTHER BAD CHOICE IN A LIFE FULL OF THEM.

HAL? HOW DID YOU...?

HAL, THERE WAS A COMPLICATION THIS AFTERNOON...

I CAME TO SEE MOM. YOU CAN TELL HER I WAS DISCHARGED, JIM. I'M *OUT* OF THE AIR FORCE.

YOU CAN TELL HER I KEPT MY PROMISE.

...MOM'S *GONE.*

WHAT? WHAT HAPPENED?

YOU KILLED HER.

JACK?

AFTER YOU *RAN AWAY,* SHE SPENT HER *LIFE* WORRYING.

SHE *HEARD* ABOUT ALL THE *CLOSE CALLS.* ALL THE *CRASHES.*

YOU KILLED MOM!

JACK! THIS IS TOUGH FOR *ALL OF US--*

SINCE WHEN IS *ANYTHING* TOUGH FOR HAL, JIM? WHEN DAD DIED *I* TOOK CARE OF MOM. I GOT A JOB TO HELP.

WHEN HAL RAN AWAY I LEFT COLLEGE. I MOVED HOME.

I GAVE MY *LIFE* FOR OUR FAMILY JUST LIKE MOM.

I WAS DAD'S SON. JIM WAS MOM'S. JACK WAS ALWAYS ON HIS OWN PATH...

WHEN HAS HAL *EVER* GIVEN THIS FAMILY *ANYTHING?*

...BUT I TOOK HIM OFF IT.

...WHERE THE HELL DO I GO FROM HERE?

THERE IS *NO ESCAPE.*

THAT IS WHY I HAVE RETURNED TO THIS FESTERING *PIT* OF A *PLANET,* QULL. I CAN HEAR THE SADISTIC *LAUGHTER* YOU DEMONS SHARE OVER THE *HORROR* THAT APPROACHES OTHERS.

I WILL *STOP* THAT HORROR. I WANT TO KNOW MORE ABOUT THE *PROPHECIES* YOU HAVE SEEN.

YOU KNOW THAT, DON'T YOU, ABIN SUR? YOU BELIEVE OUR *PROPHECIES.*

QUIET, QULL! YOU HAVE TOLD ABIN SUR *ENOUGH!*

THOSE *SECRETS* REMAIN WITH *US,* GREEN LANTERN!

I HAVE HAD *ENOUGH,* ATROCITUS!

YOU DO NOT GET TO *CHOOSE* WHEN YOU *TALK* TO ME AND WHEN YOU DO *NOT.*

AAARRG!

I WILL KNOW EVERYTHING *YOU* KNOW, DEMONS. ABOUT THE *FATE* OF THE *UNIVERSE.* ABOUT *COSMIC REVELATIONS.*

AND ABOUT "THE *BLACKEST NIGHT.*"

ACCORDING TO THE PROPHECY, EARTH IS THE *BIRTHPLACE* OF THE *BLACK*. THE *ANTITHESIS* OF THE *EMOTIONAL SPECTRUM*.

THE EMPTINESS THAT IS SAID TO *ONE DAY* CONSUME *ALL* LIGHT AND *ALL* LIFE.

"THE BLACKEST NIGHT" *AGAIN*, ABIN?

I AM *INCREASINGLY* WORRIED ABOUT YOU, MY FRIEND. YOU HAVE BECOME *OBSESSED* WITH THESE *LIES*.

AND NOW YOU FLY USING A *SHIP* RATHER THAN RELYING ON YOUR *RING*.

IT HAS BEEN *FORETOLD* MY RING WILL *FAIL* ME WHEN I MOST NEED IT.

"FORETOLD" BY THE PRISONERS OF THE PLANET *YSMAULT*. THOSE *DEMONS* WEAVE THEIR TALES IN AN ATTEMPT TO INSTILL FEAR INTO YOUR HEART AND THE *GREEN LANTERN CORPS*.

ALTHOUGH THE GUARDIANS *FORBID* FURTHER DISCUSSION, I WILL FIND *PROOF* OF THIS INEVITABLE *RISE* OF *DARKNESS*.

ATROCITUS WILL LEAD ME TO THE PLACE THAT WILL GIVE *BIRTH* TO THE *BLACK*.

I WILL ONLY LEAD YOU TO YOUR *DEATH*, GREEN LANTERN!

ATROCITUS IS IN YOUR *CUSTODY*? YOU FREED HIM FROM HIS *CRUCIFIX* ON YSMAULT? THE GUARDIANS WILL HAVE YOUR RING IF THEY DISCOVER THIS.

WISH ME *LUCK* THEN.

...ABIN...EVEN IF I AM WARY OF THE VALIDITY OF *ANY* OF THIS, YOU DO KNOW IF YOU FIND SOMETHING AND IF YOU NEED *BACKUP*...

...NOT EVEN THE GUARDIAN'S TERRITORIAL EDICT WILL KEEP ME OUT OF YOUR SECTOR.

THANK YOU, *SINESTRO*.

ABIN SUR-- GREEN LANTERN OF SPACE SECTOR 2814--

--OUT.

I WAS CAPTAIN HAL JORDAN.

NOW I WAS JUST HAL JORDAN.

DON'T LET LAMINSKI GET TO YOU, HAL.

...HAL? WHAT'RE YOU STARIN' AT?

THAT PLANE.

YEAH. TRASH HEAP'S SEEN BETTER DAYS. NOT GOOD FOR ANYTHIN' BUT PARTS.

I REMEMBER IT.

YOU REMEMBER IT?

MY DAD FLEW FOR A LOT OF AIRFIELDS IN COAST CITY. HE TOOK ME UP WITH HIM IN THAT PLANE ONCE.

LONG TIME AGO.

"DAD. I'M SCARED."

DON'T WORRY. YOU'RE FLYING WITH *ME*, SON.

YOU'VE NEVER FLOWN WITH *ME*.

I NEED TO GET BACK IN THE AIR.

MARTIN "BISHOP" JORDAN. KEN "HIGH LIFE" ARDEN. JONATHAN "HERC" STONE. CARL "ROOK" FERRIS.

THEY CALLED THEMSELVES THE FOUR MUSKETEERS WHEN THEY WERE IN THE AIR FORCE. EVENTUALLY, ALL OF THEM EXCEPT STONE LEFT TO WORK IN THE PRIVATE SECTOR.

I'D BEEN SNEAKING ONTO ARDEN'S AIRFIELD SINCE I WAS A KID.

THAT'S WHY HE CUT ME A BREAK WITH A JOB. HE KNEW DAD. HE KNEW MOM.

HE KNEW ME.

NO.

BUT I'M **TEN TIMES** THE PILOT LAMINSKI IS.

YOU'RE ALSO **TEN TIMES** AS DANGEROUS. THE PLANES YOU BROUGHT DOWN IN THE AIR FORCE DIDN'T **VANISH** OFF YOUR RECORD.

MAYBE I PUSHED IT A LITTLE. I WON'T--

PUTTING YOU BACK IN THE AIR ISN'T UP TO ME.

ONE FLIGHT.

I **SAID** IT'S NOT UP TO ME.

LOOK, I'M GETTING OLD. BUSINESS HASN'T BEEN GREAT...

...I GOT AN OFFER I COULDN'T REFUSE LAST WEEK.

I'M **SELLING** TO FERRIS AIR.

FERRIS?! YOU CAN'T BE SERIOUS.

AFTER WHAT HE **DID**... HOW COULD YOU SELL TO FERRIS?

MR. ARDEN?

I HAVE THE FINAL PAPERS. MY FATHER WOULD HAVE BROUGHT THEM HIMSELF, BUT APPARENTLY HE'S GOLFING THE GAME OF HIS *LIFE* IN PEBBLE BEACH.

IT'S *NICE* HE CAN ENJOY HIS GOLDEN YEARS.

CAROL. THIS IS HAL--

JORDAN. OF COURSE. IT'S BEEN A LONG TIME.

CAROL'S FATHER RETIRED A FEW YEARS AGO. SHE'S COME OUT OF THE COCKPIT TO RUN FERRIS AIR.

YOU'RE A PILOT?

I WAS. I HAVE MORE IMPORTANT THINGS TO DO.

LIKE *NOW*, MR. JORDAN.

HE'S A PROBLEM.

THE DEAL WAS YOU KEEP HIM ON.

MY FATHER'S NOT GOING TO LIKE THIS.

DAMMIT, DAD.

ARDEN-AIR
MECHANIC

YOU CANNOT STOP "THE BLACKEST NIGHT," GREEN LANTERN. YOU CAN ONLY *FACE* IT.

LIKE YOUR OWN *DEATH*.

I AM NOT AFRAID OF DEATH, ATROCITUS.

BUT YOU ARE *AFRAID*.

WE HAVE SHARED OUR VISION OF YOUR RING *FAILING* YOU WHEN YOU NEEDED IT MOST.

NOW YOU FLY IN A SHIP. ARMED WITH WEAPONS.

I SIMPLY REMAIN *CAUTIOUS*.

YOUR FAITH IN YOUR POWER IS *WEAKENING*.

YOU'RE *AFRAID* TO RELY ON YOUR RING. YOU DON'T BELIEVE YOUR RING IS *STRONG* ENOUGH TO SAVE YOU.

YOUR *WEAKNESS* IN YOUR OWN WILLPOWER AND YOUR POWER RING--

--CARRIES THROUGH TO YOUR *CONSTRUCTS*.

YOU FEEL FEAR...

KRRAKK

...AND I FEEL *FREEDOM!*

THE IRONY OF IT ALL. IN THE MOMENT OF DEATH, YOUR RING DID NOT FAIL *YOU*, LANTERN.

YOU FAILED *IT.*

CHNMM

N-NO.

AAARRR!

FREEDOM!

GOODBYE, GREEN LANTERN.

YOU HAVE NOT LEAPT TO FREEDOM. YOU HAVE ONLY LEAPT TO YOUR *DEATH.*

RING. WHAT IS THE SHIP'S PROJECTED POINT OF *IMPACT?*

DOWNTOWN COAST CITY, CALIFORNIA. LOSS OF LIFE ESTIMATED AT TWENTY-TWO HUNDRED AND TEN TERRESTRIALS.

THEN I CANNOT ABANDON THIS SHIP. I HAVE TO...FORCE A LANDING SOMEWHERE ELSE.

K'AA- TAANG

BOOOOMMM

>KAFF<

...RING. PREPARE MESSAGE AND FILE INFORMATION FOR SINESTRO. HE MUST CONTINUE MY MISSION. IT IS NOT ONE FOR A ROOKIE...*NNN*...

SPACE SECTOR SCAN 2814 FOR REPLACEMENT SENTIENT INITIATED.

HAL JORDAN.

WHAT--?

YOU HAVE BEEN CHOSEN.

BOOOMMMM

I AM ABIN SUR. GREEN LANTERN OF YOUR SPACE SECTOR.

SPACE SECTOR 2814.

I AM DYING.

THE BRIGHTEST DAY BECOMES THE BLACKEST NIGHT.

TO SERVE IS A GREAT HONOR.

BESTOWED UPON YOU BY THE RING.

THE RING IS FUELED BY YOUR WILLPOWER.

THE GREATEST POWER IN THE UNIVERSE.

A UNIVERSE WHERE EVIL IS CONFRONTED BY THE GREEN LANTERN CORPS.

BY THE ORDER OF THE GUARDIANS.

THE RING WILL MAKE YOUR THOUGHTS AND WISHES A REALITY.

THE GREEN LANTERN'S LIGHT MUST BE RECHARGED WITH THE POWER BATTERY.

BUT THERE IS A FLAW IN THE BATTERY, AN IMPURITY LOCATED WITHIN YOUR VISUAL SPECTRUM.

THE POWER IS INEFFECTUAL AGAINST YELLOW.

YOU HAVE BEEN CHOSEN FOR ONE REASON.

AMONG MANY OTHERS.

YOU ARE A MAN WHO CAN OVERCOME GREAT FEAR.

HAL JORDAN OF EARTH.

WHAT--?

GREEN LIGHT GRAFTED OVER MY BODY. IT WAS HOT.

WOOOSHH

BUT THE BLACK WAS AS COLD AS ICE.

I NEED SOME AIR. GOTTA GET OUT.

WILLPOWER RECOGNIZED. RING ONLINE.

WHO IS THAT? WHO'S TALK--?

ORDERS ACCEPTED.

IS THAT THE RING?

AFFIRMATIVE.

BOOOMMM

HOLY #?$%!

HOLY #?$%!

HOLY #?$%!

THERE WAS NO RUMBLING OF ANY ENGINE.

NO STICK TO PULL ON.

NO TOWER TO GET PERMISSION FROM.

IT WAS JUST ME.

ME AND THE RING.

BOOOOMM

HA HA HA HA HA HAAA!

...YOU ARE CLEAR TO OPEN ENGINE FOUR, LAMINSKI.

LAMINSKI? DO YOU COPY?

YEAH, YEAH. I COPY THAT, TOWER.

YOU HEARD THE NEWS, RIGHT? FERRIS AIR BOUGHT ARDEN OUT. CARL FERRIS--

CARL FERRIS HAS BEEN RETIRED FOR YEARS. HE'S GOT THAT SWEET LITTLE PIECE OF MEAT HE CALLS A DAUGHTER RUNNING HIS AIRFIELDS.

WITHIN A WEEK, I'LL BE TEACHIN' HER A NEW MEANING FOR THE TERM "LANDING STRIP--"

LAMINSKI? LAMINSKI, WHAT THE HELL WAS THAT?

I... I DON'T...

TEN TIMES THE PILOT.

YOU'RE LOSING CONTROL! LAMINSKI?!

LOSE YOUR COOL AT FIFTEEN THOUSAND FEET--

--PAY THE PRICE. C'MON, LAMINSKI.

STEADY.

STEADY NOW.

WHAT THE HELL HAPPENED, TOM?

I SAW SOMETHING GLOWING, MR. ARDEN. SOMETHING *GREEN*.

OW.

SENTIENTS APPROACHING.

CONCEALING IDENTITY.

Hnn.

STOP *DOING* THAT.

WHOA.

Um. Hi.

YOUR PILOT MIGHT, uh, NEED SOME MEDICAL ATTENTION. I THINK I HEARD HIM THROW UP.

WHO THE HECK ARE YOU?

GREEN LANTERN OF SPACE SECTOR 2814.

GREEN... LANTERN?

WHAT'S A "GREEN LANTERN"?

KLUK

I'M CURIOUS WHAT A "GREEN LANTERN" IS MYSELF, CAROL.

YOU'RE NOT TRYING TO STEAL MY GIRL, ARE YOU, SUPER-HERO?

CAROL HADN'T LOOKED UP FROM HER ACCOUNTING BOOKS IN YEARS.

SHE'D FORGOTTEN WHY SHE EVER DID.

Ah-HEM.

A LIFE TURNED UPSIDE DOWN.

I'M SURE MISS FERRIS APPRECIATES THE CATCH, BUT YOU CAN LET GO OF HER NOW.

RIGHT.

RIGHT.

A DYING ALIEN.

A WISHING RING.

THE GLOW OF THE UNIFORM KEPT THEM BLINDED ENOUGH. THEY DIDN'T RECOGNIZE ME BEHIND THE MASK.

AT LEAST, MOST OF THEM.

WHERE'D THOSE GIANT GREEN HANDS THAT WERE HOLDING THE PLANE GO? HOW'D YOU DO THAT?

CONSTRUCT MANIFESTATION TRIGGERED BY FORCE OF WILL.

WILL YOU SHUT UP?!

SILENT MODE ACTIVATED.

YOU ACT AS IF YOU BARELY KNOW WHAT'S HAPPENING YOURSELF.

I'M A SCIENTIST. I SPECIALIZE IN ASTROPHYSICS, ALTERNATIVE FUEL SOURCES AND THEORETICAL FUTURE-SCIENCE.

PERHAPS I CAN BE OF ASSISTANCE.

TRUTHFULLY, I DIDN'T KNOW WHAT I WAS DOING.

BUT I'D FIGURE IT OUT MYSELF.

NO, THANKS.

THAT'S WHAT I ALWAYS DID.

WHO IS HE?

WHERE'D HE COME FROM?

ARE YOU ALL RIGHT, CAROL?

CAROL.

I APPRECIATE YOUR CONCERN, DR. HAMMOND, BUT *ONE* DINNER DOES NOT MAKE ME "YOUR GIRL."

YOU'RE AN *EMPLOYEE.*

AND I'VE MADE IT CRYSTAL CLEAR. I DON'T *DATE* EMPLOYEES.

I'M *NOT* AN EMPLOYEE. I'M A *CONSULTANT.*

YOU CAN'T TREAT ME LIKE YOU DO *EVERYONE ELSE.* FERRIS AIR ISN'T THE *ONLY* COMPANY I WORK--

VEETVEET

TELL YOUR FATHER "HELLO."

WHO WAS HE?

I ASKED THE SAME QUESTIONS EVERYONE AT FERRIS DID.

ABOUT THIS ALIEN.

HE WAS OBVIOUSLY SOME KIND OF SOLDIER OR OFFICER.

I WASN'T GOING TO LEAVE HIM OUT IN THE OPEN.

HE DESERVED BETTER THAN THAT.

NO MATTER WHO HE WAS.

THE GREEN LANTERN? IS THAT WHAT *THIS* IS?

RING? RING, YOU CAN *TALK* NOW.

THIS IS YOUR POWER BATTERY.

POWER BATTERY? WHAT'S A POWER BATTER--

HEY!

A GREEN LANTERN'S POWER BATTERY IS THEIR POWER RING'S CHARGING STATION. RECHARGING REQUIRED APPROXIMATELY EVERY TWENTY-FOUR TERRESTRIAL HOURS.

LET GO, DAMMIT!

INCORRECT OATH.

KLANK

POWER LEVELS 100%.

GREEN LANTERN OF SPACE SECTOR 2814.

YOU WILL REPORT TO OA FOR TRAINING IMMEDIATELY.

WHAT?

HAVE A NICE FLIGHT.

WHERE THE **HELL** AM I?

THE PLANET OA. CENTRAL PRECINCT OF THE GREEN LANTERN CORPS.

AND HOME TO THE **GUARDIANS** OF THE UNIVERSE-- IMMORTAL WATCHERS AND PROTECTORS OF ALL.

ABIN?

DISENGAGING AUTOPILOT.

WAIT. WHY DID YOU BRING ME HERE? WHAT AM I SUPPOSED TO DO NOW?

HELLO?!

TUTORIAL OFF.

SSLAATTT

HAHAJAHAHAH

IS THAT A **HUMAN**?

A **HUMAN** GREEN LANTERN?

WHAT'S A **HUMAN**?

THAT'S NO WAY TA TREAT YOUR **BATTERY**.

NICE LANDIN', POOZER.

NAME'S KILOWOG.

WELCOME TA RINGSLINGIN' 101. OR AS KE'HAAN AND I LIKE TO CALL IT--

--THE WORST DAY A' YOUR WORTHLESS LIFE!

OH, I GET IT.

THIS IS BOOT CAMP.

GET IN LINE WITH THE REST OF THE WHITE CIRCLES.

SHOOOM

IT'S WHERE YOU PRIMORDIAL QUADRUPEDS BELONG.

YOU WANNA BOX?

THEY WERE TRACKING IT WHEN IT FLEW PAST MARS.

BUT IT WASN'T UNTIL IT *TURNED* TOWARD EARTH THAT IT WAS RED FLAGGED.

SOMETHING BROKE OFF WHEN IT ENTERED THE ATMOSPHERE. RIGHT ABOVE BIG BEAR, CALIFORNIA.

FORT ROCK'S SENT A UNIT TO INVESTIGATE THE SECOND CRASH SITE. WE'RE HANDLING THIS ONE.

WHAT IS IT, MAJOR STONE? A FALLEN SPY SATELLITE? A METEOR?

YOU'RE THE SCIENTIST THAT SPECIALIZES IN THE THEORETICAL, DR. HAMMOND.

YOU TELL US.

MY GOD...

THE RING CAN MAKE WHATEVER *TOOL* YA NEED. JUST GOTTA PICTURE IT IN YOUR MIND. *WILL* IT TO *LIFE*.

FORCE FIELDS. ENERGY BEAMS.

EVERYONE SEE THAT?

YES, SIR.

YOU PRACTICE *WELL*, AHTIER. WHY DO YOU SPEAK SO *LITTLE*?

BECAUSE I *FEAR* MY *DUTY*, KE'HAAN.

GREEN LANTERNS BURN *BRIGHT*, BUT THEY BURN OUT *QUICKLY*.

IF THAT *HUMAN* CAN MAKE IT, SO CAN *YOU*.

THANKS FOR THE RIDE, BUT I'LL GET OFF HERE.

KRSHH

YOU *WILLED* YOURSELF FREE, EARTHMAN...

...NOW TRY CATCHIN' *THIS.*

NnNGg

WHAT THE HELL HAPPENED?

WHAT DO YOU MEAN WHAT HAPPENED, HUMAN? IT WAS *YELLOW.*

EVERYONE IN THE UNIVERSE KNOWS A GREEN LANTERN'S POWER RING IS *INEFFECTUAL* AGAINST *YELLOW.*

HE DON'T KNOW NOTHIN' 'BOUT THE CORPS, CH'P. HE'S FROM *EARTH.*

ASK ME, KILOWOG, EARTH'S A BACKWARD WORLD BEST LEFT TO THEIR *OWN.*

WHY *YELLOW?*

WHAT?

WHY WOULD THESE RINGS NOT BE ABLE TO AFFECT ANYTHING *YELLOW?*

YOU DON'T ASK QUESTIONS IN THE CORPS. YOU DO YOUR *DUTY.*

I DON'T EVEN KNOW WHAT THAT *"DUTY"* IS.

NOW DON'T GET ALL *PUFFY CHESTED* AGAIN. NEXT TIME, I WON'T BE SO NICE.

"TO SERVE AND PROTECT YOUR RESPECTIVE SECTORS AND ALL LIFE WITHIN THEM."

KILOWOG.

LET ME SPEAK WITH THE EARTHMAN.

WHAT BUSINESS IS HE OF YOURS, TOMAR?

HE'S WEARING *ABIN SUR'S* RING.

MY NAME IS *TOMAR-RE* OF XUDAR. GREEN LANTERN OF SPACE SECTOR 2815.

BY ALL ACCOUNTS, I AM YOUR *NEIGHBOR.*

I'M HAL JORDAN.

ABIN SUR'S REPLACEMENT IN THE CORPS. MY RING IS UNABLE TO *UNLOCK* HIS LOG...HOW DID HE DIE?

HE CRASHED HIS SHIP IN THE DESERT.

HIS *SHIP?*

HE DIDN'T *NEED* THAT SHIP.

THEN WHY WAS HE FLYING ONE?

HE DID WHAT NO GREEN LANTERN SHOULD. HE ALLOWED HIMSELF TO FEEL *FEAR.*

AND IT HAPPENED BECAUSE ABIN SUR DISOBEYED THE GUARDIAN'S TERRITORIAL EDICT AND PURSUED AN ENEMY *OUTSIDE* OF HIS SECTOR.

HE CAME INTO CONFLICT WITH A GROUP KNOWN AS THE EMPIRE OF TEARS.

AFTERWARD, HE GREW INCREASINGLY *PARANOID.*

HE BECAME *OBSESSED* WITH *DOOMSDAY PROPHECIES* AND *PRISMS.*

FRACTURED LIGHT. SPLINTERED SOULS. NOTHING MADE SENSE.

NOTHING MAKES SENSE TO ME RIGHT NOW.

THIS IS THE **BOOK** OF **OA.** IN IT-- TALES OF THE GREEN LANTERN CORPS.

ABIN SUR'S TALE IS NOW AMONG THEM. AN ENDING **TRAGIC.**

ONE DAY **YOUR** TALE WILL BE HERE TOO, AS WILL MINE.

A WORD OF ADVICE, SUCCESSOR.

IF YOU NEED HELP--

--ASK FOR IT.

THE SUN NEVER SET.

YER SUPPOSED TA FLY *AROUND* THEM, JORDAN, NOT *THROUGH* THEM!

I DIDN'T KNOW HOW LONG I GOT MY ASS HANDED TO ME.

I'LL DO IT.

YOU WON'T DO IT.

IT'S JUST A *COLOR*.

DAYS.

YOU MISHANDLE YOUR POWER BATTERY AGAIN, HAL JORDAN, AND SHORM WILL MISHANDLE *YOU*.

UNDERSTOOD, SALAAK.

YOU STILL GOT *CRACKS* IN YOUR CONSTRUCTS, JORDAN--

--BUT IT AIN'T BAD.

A WEEK?

YA DIDN'T DO IT *GRACEFULLY* AND YA DIDN'T DO IT *EASY*, BUT AS FAR AS I'M CONCERNED YER NOT COMPLETELY *USELESS.*

YOU *EARNED* YOUR *BADGES.*

SO LET'S LIGHT 'EM UP!

IN BRIGHTEST DAY IN BLACKEST NIGHT

IN BRIGHTEST DAY...IN BLACKEST NIGHT

NO EVIL SHALL ESCAPE MY SIGHT

NO EVIL SHALL ESCAPE MY SIGHT

LET THOSE WHO WORSHIP EVIL'S MIGHT...

LET THOSE WHO WORSHIP EVIL'S MIGHT

WHY WAS I NOT NOTIFIED IMMEDIATELY, GUARDIAN?

YOU WERE ENGAGED IN BATTLE WITH THE MANHUNTERS. WE DID NOT WANT YOUR FOCUS DISRUPTED.

RIDICULOUS. WHEN HAS MY FOCUS *EVER* BEEN DISRUPTED?

IT IS TRUE. YOUR RECORD IS FAR SUPERIOR TO THAT OF YOUR FELLOW OFFICERS. YOUR SECTOR IS NEARLY CLEAN OF THE CHAOS THAT ONCE CLAIMED IT.

YOU HAVE BEEN CALLED THE "GREATEST" BY MANY.

...HAVE I?

THAT IS WHY I ASK YOU TO VENTURE TO EARTH WHERE YOU WILL CONTACT ABIN SUR'S REPLACEMENT AND INVESTIGATE THE CIRCUMSTANCES INVOLVING HIS DEATH.

WHAT OF PROPER PROTOCOL? SALAAK HAS NOT DOWNLOADED THE OFFICIAL MISSION TO MY RING, GUARDIAN.

THIS MISSION WILL STAY BETWEEN US. AND YOU CAN CALL ME GANTHET.

GANTHET? WHY HAVE YOU TAKEN A NAME WHEN NO *OTHER* GUARDIANS HAVE?

SO THAT YOU *KNOW* ME.

GREEN LANTERNS *PARTNERING* UP? THIS GOES AGAINST YOUR *TERRITORIAL* EDICT.

I AM ASKING YOU TO BREAK THAT EDICT--

--FOR YOUR MENTOR AND FRIEND.

WELL THEN, *GANTHET...*

HAS ANYONE SEEN DR. HAMMOND?

...THIS IS THE *SIXTH* MESSAGE I'VE *LEFT*, CAROL.

YOU CALL ME *BACK* AND WE CAN SMOOTH ALL OF THIS *TENSION* OUT OVER *DINNER*--

--OR YOU CAN CONSIDER MY *ENDORSEMENT* OF FERRIS AIR'S AERONAUTICS *VOIDED*. ON TOP OF EVERYTHING *ELSE* THAT'S HAPPENED THIS WEEK, I'M SURE YOU AND YOUR FATHER DON'T NEED *THAT*.

DR. HAMMOND.

WHAT IS IT?

IT TOOK US A FEW DAYS, BUT WE'VE FINALLY DISASSEMBLED THE ALIEN CRAFT'S THRUSTERS.

WHAT?

WE'VE DISASSEMBLED THE THRUSTERS. WE CAN REACH THE FUEL CHAMBERS, BUT WE'RE HESITANT ABOUT OPENING--

HESITANT? USE YOUR *COMMON SENSE.*

YOUR HELMET, DR. HAMMOND--

DO YOU *HEAR* THAT? THE FUEL CHAMBER'S *EMPTY.*

LIKE YOUR HEADS.

HONGG HONGG

YOU SEE?

THERE'S NOTHING TO BE *AFRAID* OF.

FSSSSSS

CLOSE THE DOOR!

WHAT IS IT?

THE SHIP'S FUEL ISN'T A *LIQUID!* IT'S POWERED BY SOME KIND OF *ROCK!*

LOOKS LIKE A METEOR.

GET HAMMOND CLEAR!

HE'S GOING INTO CONVULSIONS!

NnNNnNNn!

HAMMOND'S SO *CREEPY.*

WH-WHAT DID YOU SAY?

MEDIC! WE NEED A MEDIC!

LOOKS LIKE HE'S ALL RIGHT. TOO BAD.

GOD, I HOPE HE'S ALL RIGHT.

THAT MUSTACHE MAKES HIM LOOK LIKE A PEDOPHILE.

WHAT'S WRONG WITH HIS HEAD?

HECTOR HAMMOND IS A LOSER.

TERRIBLE TASTE IN SUITS.

HE'S ALWAYS CALLING CAROL FERRIS. LIKE SOME KIND OF STALKER.

SHUT UP.

HIS BREATH IS TERRIBLE.

WAS CHARGING MY POWER RING ON AN ALIEN WORLD. GRADUATING FROM AN INTERGALACTIC BOOT CAMP.

AS SOON AS I WAS DONE, I WAS COVERED IN GREEN LIGHT. I WAS TOLD MY RING WOULD ALERT ME TO ANY EXTRATERRESTRIAL INCIDENTS I SHOULD INTERVENE IN.

THEN I WAS SHIPPED BACK HOME.

HAL?

TOM?

I CAN'T BELIEVE IT! YOU'RE THE *GREEN LANTERN!*

ANY LIFE OUTSIDE THE CORPS WASN'T TAKEN INTO CONSIDERATION.

THE...GREEN LANTERN?

WHAT ARE YOU, *UH,* TALKING ABOUT?

WELL, YOU'RE WEARING A GLOWING GREEN *RING.*

AND THERE'S *THIS.*

WHAT DO YOU MEAN YOU'RE NOT A SUPER-HERO?

YOU *CAUGHT* LAMINSKI'S PLANE LAST WEEK!

ANYONE ELSE WOULD'VE DONE THE SAME IF THEY *COULD*.

EVEN IF HE *IS* A JERK.

WELL, YOU'RE NOT GONNA HAVE TO WORRY ABOUT *HIM* ANYMORE.

I'M NOT SUPPOSED TO USE THE RING TO SORT OUT *PERSONAL PROBLEMS*, TOM.

NO, I MEAN THE *WALKOUT*.

WHAT WALKOUT?

KLANG

SEE ALL THE *EMPTY* LOCKERS?

ONCE WORD SPREAD THAT CAROL "LADY" FERRIS WAS TAKING THE REINS FROM MR. ARDEN, NO ONE WAS PARTICULARLY *EXCITED*.

AND AFTER HER FATHER DIDN'T SHOW FOR THE BIG *COMPANY SPEECH*, SHE HAD TO GIVE IT HERSELF--

--AFTERWARDS JUST ABOUT EVERYONE *QUIT*.

...OF COURSE, I'D MAKE IT WORTH YOUR TIME, MR. TRAINOR. PLENTY OF PAY AND BENEFITS AND A SHARE IN THE PROFITS...

...IF YOU KNOW OF ANY OTHER *PILOTS* THAT YOU'D LIKE FLYING ALONGSIDE YOU...

MY FATHER'S STILL TRAVELING. HE'LL BE OUT OF THE COUNTRY THE REST OF THE...

YES, OF COURSE, HE WOULD'VE MADE THE CALL HIMSELF IF HE COULD, BUT...

MR. TRAINOR, LISTEN TO ME. THIS IS THE OPPORTUNITY OF A... MR. TRAINOR?

...LARRY?

NOK NOK

YES?

MISS FERRIS.

MR. JORDAN? WHAT ARE YOU DOING HERE?

I JUST WANTED TO THROW IN MY RESIGNATION ALONG WITH THE REST.

YOU HAVEN'T SHOWN YOUR FACE HERE ALL *WEEK.* I ASSUMED YOU ALREADY HAD.

YOU ASSUMED RIGHT. I GUESS I WANTED TO MAKE IT *OFFICIAL.*

AND IF YOUR *FATHER* WAS HERE--

WHAT?

WHAT WOULD YOU *DO* IF MY FATHER *WAS* HERE?

I'D TELL HIM WHAT I'VE BEEN WANTING TO FOR *YEARS.*

I'D TELL HIM EVERYTHING MY MOTHER *BEGGED* ME *NOT* TO.

YOU KNOW WHAT, JORDAN? LET'S MAKE THIS DAY EVEN *BETTER* THAN IT *HAS* BEEN.

TELL *ME.*

YOUR FATHER PUT *MINE* IN A *DEATH TRAP!*

HE SAVED A FEW *BUCKS* AND HE SENT HIM OFF IN A PLANE THAT NEVER HAD A *CHANCE* AT *LANDING.*

AND NOW, WHILE *MY* DAD IS *ROTTING* IN THE *GROUND,* YOURS IS PLAYING *PUTT-PUTT* ON THE GULF OF THE MEXICO, DRINKING A MARGARITA AND PROBABLY SMOKING A CIGAR THAT COSTS MORE THAN WHAT I MAKE IN A DAY!

YOU DON'T MAKE *ANYTHING*, JORDAN. YOU JUST *QUIT*, REMEMBER?

NOW IS THAT *ALL* YOU'VE GOT TO *BARK* ABOUT?

FORGET IT, "LADY" FERRIS. I'LL SAVE THE REST FOR *HIM* WHEN HE'S *BACK* FROM HIS EXTENDED *HOLIDAY*.

DO YOU WANT TO FLY AGAIN?

WHAT?

DO YOU WANT TO FLY AGAIN?

YES.

BUT NOT *HERE*.

THEN *WHERE*?

WHO'S GOING TO HIRE YOU?

AFTER EVERYTHING YOU'VE DONE, *WHO'S* GOING TO TAKE THAT *RISK*?

I DIDN'T NEED A PLANE TO FLY ANYMORE.

THE RING MADE IT EASY.

THE RING MADE IT TOO EASY.

PLEASE, HAL.

I NEED A PILOT. AND YOU NEED A PLANE.

FOR A SPLIT SECOND, I DIDN'T SEE THE SHARK I THOUGHT SHE WAS. I SAW THE LITTLE GIRL I'D MET ALL THAT TIME AGO.

SHE CRIED LOUDER THAN I DID WHEN MY FATHER'S PLANE CRASHED.

SOMEHOW I'D FORGOTTEN THAT.

I OFFER SACRIFICE FOR THE *PROPHECIES* CONTAINED WITHIN THE *LIQUID* OF *LIFE*.

I ASK FOR THE *NAME* OF THE BEING THAT WILL *BIRTH* THE *BLACK*.

HEAR MY *CRIES*, TASTE THIS *FLESH* AND GRANT ME A GLIMPSE OF *TOMORROW*.

WITH BLOOD AND RAGE OF CRIMSON RED

RIPPED FROM A CORPSE SO FRESHLY DEAD

TOGETHER WITH OUR HELLISH HATE

WE'LL BURN YOU ALL, THAT IS YOUR FATE!

THIS BEING HOLDS THE POWER.

WILLIAM... HAND.

IT FELT GOOD TO FLY.

BUT IN THE BACK OF MY HEAD, I KNEW I WAS FLYING FOR THE WRONG PERSON.

I CONVINCED MYSELF I WAS ONLY STAYING UNTIL CARL FERRIS CAME BACK.

UNTIL I FINALLY GOT AN ANSWER TO THE QUESTION I'VE ASKED MYSELF A MILLION TIMES OVER.

HOW COULD HE LIVE THE WAY HE DOES AFTER WHAT HAPPENED?

HOW COULD HE SHIRK THE RESPONSIBILITY?

I TRIED TO STAY ANGRY IN THE AIR, BUT IT WAS HARD.

THE OPEN SKY INVITING ME BACK IN. AND CAROL FERRIS...

...WHY COULDN'T I STOP THINKING ABOUT HER?

CAROL.

FERRIS WANTS THIS ONE PRECISE, JORDAN. WE'RE ABOUT ROBUST TRAJECTORY TRACKING TODAY, NOT SPLIT-S MANEUVERS.

I WAS JUST LOOSENING UP.

WHAT HAPPENED TO THAT GIRL?

I DON'T KNOW IF THIS IS SUCH A GOOD IDEA, MISS FERRIS.

HE'S WANDERING ALL OVER THE PLACE. IF HE STARTS SOME OF HIS HOTDOGGING--

THIS IS HIS LAST CHANCE.

HE CAN'T SCREW IT UP.

VROOOM

WHAT IS THAT IMBECILE DOING?

FLYING WITHOUT HIS POWER RING.

WITHOUT HIS...? RING. LOCATE HIS POWER RING.

"THIS MAVERICK NEEDS A LESSON IN RESPONSIBILITY.

"BRING HIS RING TO ME."

WHOA!

HEY.

I'VE GOT SOMETHING AT TWELVE O'CLOCK. THOUGHT I WAS ALONE UP HERE.

NOTHING ON OUR SCREEN. ARE YOU SURE?

VEEP VEEP VEEP

JORDAN?

COME IN, JORDAN.

BOOM

...WHO'S GOING TO SHELL OUT THE *TWENTY MILLION* DOLLARS FOR THAT JET?

I DON'T *SEE* ANY *POCKETS.*

YOUR *TERRESTRIAL AFFAIRS* SHOULD BE OF *LITTLE* CONCERN, EARTHMAN. YOU ARE IN THE PRESENCE OF A *VETERAN.*

NEVER QUESTION A *SUPERIOR OFFICER.*

NEVER CHALLENGE THOSE MORE *POWERFUL* THAN *YOU.*

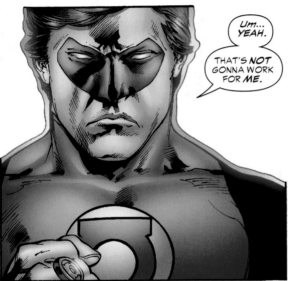

Um... YEAH.

THAT'S *NOT* GONNA WORK FOR *ME.*

DO YOU HAVE *ANY* IDEA WHAT YOU JUST *DID?* WHAT YOU JUST *COST* ME?

RING. CAN YOU *REBUILD* THE PLANE?

THE QUESTION SHOULDN'T BE POSED TO YOUR *RING,* IT SHOULD BE POSED TO *YOU.*

WHAT DOES KILOWOG TEACH YOU WHITE CIRCLES THESE DAYS?

HE TAUGHT ME THAT MY *DUTY* WAS TO LOCATE ANY *ALIENS* CAUSING *TROUBLE* AND KICK THEM *OFF* PLANET.

YOUR CONSTRUCTS ARE *WEAK.*

THEY'RE LACED WITH *ANGER.*

AND ALTHOUGH THE GUARDIANS BELIEVE *FEAR* CREATES *CRACKS* IN OUR *WILLPOWER--*

--ANGER WILL *DISTORT* IT.

ANGER WILL MAKE IT *UNFOCUSED.*

A GREEN LANTERN *NEEDS* TO BE *FOCUSED.*

I NEED TO GO.

GO? GO WHERE?

BACK TO MY *REAL* JOB.

YOU NEED MORE *TRAINING,* ROOKIE.

WHAT THE HELL ARE YOU DOING HERE *ANYWAY?* TOMAR-RE TOLD ME ALL OF US ARE SUPPOSED TO STAY IN OUR *OWN* SECTOR.

YES, THE GUARDIANS' TERRITORIAL EDICT DISSUADES FRATERNIZING AMONG THE CORPS.

BUT I HAVE MY ORDERS. AND THEY ARE FROM A MUCH *HIGHER* AUTHORITY THAN TOMAR-RE.

I'VE BEEN DISPATCHED TO THIS PRIMITIVE PLANET PLAGUED WITH POLITICAL BORDERS AND TERRESTRIAL WAR TO INVESTIGATE THE DEATH OF YOUR PREDECESSOR.

ABIN SUR CRASHED HIS SHIP IN THE CALIFORNIA DESERT.

WHY?

I DON'T KNOW. HE DIDN'T TELL--

GREEN LANTERN OF SPACE SECTOR 1417--MESSAGE FROM GREEN LANTERN 2814 WAITING.

WHAT? WHAT DID YOUR RING SAY?

I DON'T KNOW. MAYBE YOURS IS SCREWING WITH IT.

MESSAGE WAITING.

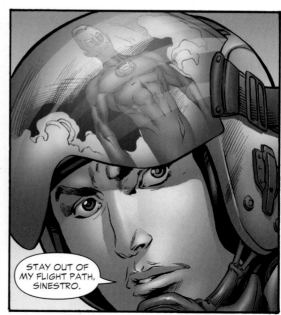

STAY OUT OF MY FLIGHT PATH, SINESTRO.

I DON'T BELIEVE IT.

WHAT?

LOOK.

EEERRRTT

OH, BOY.

WHAT THE HELL WAS *THAT?*

IT'S NOT WHAT IT LOOKS LIKE.

IT LOOKS LIKE YOU'RE PLAYING *GAMES,* MR. JORDAN.

PURPOSELY FLYING BELOW RADAR, REFUSING TO COMMUNICATE.

CAROL--

I MUST'VE BEEN *CRAZY* TO THINK THIS WAS A GOOD IDEA.

YOU'RE NOT *INSANE,* CAROL.

IN FACT, YOU HAVE QUITE A *BEAUTIFUL* MIND.

AMONG *OTHER* THINGS.

H-HECTOR?

OH MY GOD. WHAT'S HAPPENING?

WHAT'S HAPPENING? I CAN READ YOUR THOUGHTS.

DON'T *TOUCH* ME!

DON'T YOU SEE, MY DEAR, WHAT A WONDERFUL *CONNECTION* WE CAN HAVE NOW.

DEEPER THAN ANYTHING *ANYONE* HAS.

OUR MINDS WILL BE *ONE*.

AND OUR... OUR...

YOU...

...OH, THIS IS WONDERFUL.

WHAT *UNIQUE* EXPERIENCES *THIS* ONE HAS.

HAL JORDAN. I SEE YOUR LIFE.

WHAT A *LIFE*--

--GREEN LANTERN!

...REVENGE WILL BE MINE.

COAST CITY
66 miles

COAST CITY.

HAND MORTUARY

ROOM 5

R

WILLIAM.

HAN MOR

YOUR FATHER JUST FINISHED CLEANING THIS ONE UP!

I WASN'T D-D-DOING ANYTHING, MOM! I SWEAR!

HOW MANY TIMES HAVE WE TOLD YOU TO STAY OUT OF THE BASEMENT?

I KNOW, BUT...I JUST WANTED TO L-L-LOOK.

WHY? WHY CAN'T YOU BE A GOOD CHRISTIAN LIKE YOUR BROTHERS?

I DON'T KNOW.

YOU HAVE MET EXTRA-TERRESTRIALS.

LIFE FAR BEYOND OURS.

THEY GAVE YOU A POWER RING. A BAND OF ENERGY AND WILL.

THEY CALLED IT THE GREATEST WEAPON IN THE UNIVERSE.

THE GREATEST TECHNOLOGY.

HA HA HA HA HA!

GIVE ME THIS EMERALD MIRACLE, HAL JORDAN. GIVE...

...NO.

NO, YOU CAN'T HAVE HER.

NO. CAROL FERRIS IS MINE.

CHRISTINE FERRIS
Loving Wife and Mother

MAT

SHE'S MINE!

I DON'T... WANT HER, HAMMOND.

YOU HAVE MET **EXTRA-TERRESTRIALS.**

LIFE FAR **BEYOND** OURS.

THEY GAVE YOU A **POWER RING.** A BAND OF **ENERGY** AND **WILL.**

THEY CALLED IT THE GREATEST **WEAPON** IN THE UNIVERSE.

THE GREATEST **TECHNOLOGY.**

HA HA HA HA HA!

GIVE ME THIS **EMERALD MIRACLE,** HAL JORDAN. GIVE...

...NO.

NO, YOU CAN'T HAVE **HER.**

CHRISTINE FERRIS
Loving Wife and Mother

NO, **CAROL FERRIS** IS MINE.

SHE'S **MINE!**

I DON'T... **WANT** HER, HAMMOND.

LIAR!

KRRRAKKKK

I SEE YOUR THOUGHTS FLOATING *AROUND* YOU. EVERY LAYER OF *WHO* YOU *ARE* PEELED BACK AND ON *DISPLAY.*

I SEE THINGS NO ONE *ELSE* SEES.

YOU'VE LIVED YOUR *LIFE* TRYING TO PROVE TO EVERYONE THE *DEATH* OF YOUR FATHER DIDN'T MAKE YOU *AFRAID.*

IT'S MADE IT SO *EXCITING.*

BUT YOU HAVEN'T SHARED IT WITH *ANYONE.*

UNTIL *NOW.*

I TRIED TO POUR SOME WILL INTO THE RING, BUT IT FELT LIKE IT WAS SLIPPING OFF.

THE BEST I COULD DO –

-- WAS BLIND HIM.

AAAAaaHH!

CAROL?

H-HAL?

HAL, WHAT'S GOING ON?

YOUR BOYFRIEND'S BACK.

HE'S *NOT* MY BOYFRIEND.

LOOK AT THAT SHARED *TRAUMA*.

ALL THE *TRAGEDY* IN YOUR LIFE, IT'S NO WONDER YOU'RE *BOTH* SO *COLD*.

BUT *YOU* DON'T HAVE TO BE, CAROL. IT'S *YOUR* CHOICE.

YOU ARE ALSO BREAKING THIRTY-FOUR TERRESTRIAL AND INTERGALACTIC LAWS.

CHIEF AMONG THEM, HUMAN, IS ATTACKING AN OFFICER OF THE GREEN LANTERN CORPS.

EVEN IF I DO USE THE TERM *"OFFICER"* LOOSELY.

WHAT?

RING. **REMOVE** HIS AIR SUPPLY.

APPROXIMATELY FIVE SECONDS UNTIL THE AIR FROM HIS LUNGS IS EVACUATED.

N-NO. WHO...?

THREE.

ONE.

ASTONISHING.

A RUDIMENTARY TELEPATH LIKE THAT ACTUALLY *DISRUPTED* YOUR CONCENTRATION?

GREEN... LANTERN?

COME, ROOKIE.

WOOOSHH

HSSSHH

...HAL?

YOU WILL CONTAIN THIS POWER OF THE BLACK FOR MY JOURNEY *HOME.*

NOW TAKE ME TO ITS HOST.

KRIK

TAKE ME TO *WILLIAM HAND.*

KRIK
KRIK
KRIK
KRIK

...**REMOVING** THE AIR FROM HIS **LUNGS** WAS A **SIMPLE** SOLUTION. WITHOUT IT, HIS TELEKINETIC BRAIN HAD NO **CHOICE** BUT TO SHUT **DOWN**.

I WOULD'VE THOUGHT OF THAT.

I DON'T THINK YOU THINK OF **ANYTHING**, JORDAN. DO YOU **EVER** PLAN AHEAD?

FOR EXAMPLE: **FLYING** TODAY.

IF I HAD NOT BROUGHT YOU YOUR RING, YOU WOULD HAVE **DIED**.

AND YOU WOULD'VE BEEN A **MURDERER**. **YOU** WERE THE ONE IN MY **FLIGHT** PATH.

WHY WOULD YOU EVEN FLY **WITHOUT** YOUR RING?

SOMEHOW, I DOUBT THAT.

I FORGOT IT.

FINE. LESSON **LEARNED**. CAN YOU **GO** NOW? I'VE HAD ALL THE **TRAINING** I NEED.

KILOWOG TAUGHT ME HOW TO RING SLING.

POORLY.

SALAAK HAD ME TEST THE CHARGING LIMITATIONS.

SALAAK'S "**TESTS**" ARE WORTHLESS WHEN FACED WITH THE **REALITY** OF A "**DEAD**" RING.

AND **EVERYONE** WARNED ME ABOUT THE YELLOW IMPURITY.

OF COURSE, NO ONE CAN ACTUALLY TELL ME **WHAT** THAT IS OR **WHY** IT'S THERE.

IT DOESN'T EVEN MAKE ANY SENSE.

YELLOW.

Hh.

WHAT?

I HAVE BEEN ATTEMPTING TO SEEK THE TRUTH ABOUT THE YELLOW IMPURITY FOR YEARS. I WAS SUSPENDED AFTER ACCUSING THE GUARDIANS OF PUTTING IT THERE THEMSELVES WHEN **I** WAS A ROOKIE.

DID YOU KNOW HIM?

ABIN SUR WAS *MY* MENTOR.

I SUPPOSE I QUESTIONED HIM AND DISRESPECTED HIM AS MUCH AS YOU DO ME.

HE SHOWED ME HOW TO TEMPER THAT. AND WHY IT WAS NECESSARY FOR A MEMBER OF THE GREEN LANTERN CORPS.

SO HE TOLD YOU TO SHUT UP AND PLAY GOOD SOLDIER?

OF COURSE NOT. I AM AN INDIVIDUALISTIC THINKER, AS YOU ARE. I'D NEVER BELONGED TO A GROUP LIKE THE CORPS BEFORE.

SO I HAD NEVER LEARNED HOW TO *TRUST* THE BEINGS AROUND ME.

IN PART, THAT'S WHERE MY QUESTIONING CAME FROM.

HE HELPED ME LEARN TO TRUST MY FELLOW CORPSMAN. THANKFULLY, IT DIDN'T CHANGE MY DRIVE TO SEEK THE TRUTH OR MY DETERMINATION TO ARGUE AGAINST THE THEOLOGIES I DISAGREE WITH.

THEN WHAT *DID* IT HELP YOU DO, SINESTRO?

SINESTRO. GREEN LANTERN 1417 REGISTERED IN DIRECT VICINITY. MESSAGE 22 UNLOCKED.

I REALIZE I HAVE NOT BEEN AS RIGHTEOUS AND EFFECTIVE AN OFFICER LIKE YOU OF LATE.

BUT THIS TEACHER FEARS **NOT BEING** SURPASSED BY HIS STUDENT.

YOUR SUCCESS IS ALL I **HOPE** FOR, SINESTRO.

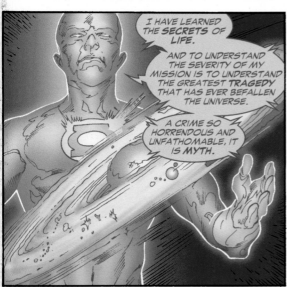

I HAVE LEARNED THE **SECRETS** OF LIFE.

AND TO UNDERSTAND THE SEVERITY OF MY MISSION IS TO UNDERSTAND THE GREATEST **TRAGEDY** THAT HAS EVER BEFALLEN THE UNIVERSE.

A CRIME SO HORRENDOUS AND UNFATHOMABLE, IT IS MYTH.

LONG BEFORE THE GUARDIANS OF THE UNIVERSE RECRUITED SENTIENT LIFE FORMS INTO THE GREEN LANTERN CORPS, THEY CREATED A DIFFERENT POLICE FORCE.

ONE THEY BELIEVED WOULD NEVER BE MANIPULATED BY EMOTION. THE GUARDIANS SAW EMOTION AS A WEAKNESS IN INTELLIGENT LIFE.

THEY CONSTRUCTED THOUSANDS OF ARTIFICIAL SOLDIERS. MANHUNTERS. THEY DISPATCHED THEM ACROSS THE UNIVERSE TO MAINTAIN ORDER.

FOR EONS, THEY DID JUST THAT.

UNTIL THE MASSACRE.

"THERE WERE FIVE SURVIVORS.

"FIVE WITHIN AN ENTIRE SECTOR ONCE FULL OF LIFE."

THOSE FIVE BECAME KNOWN AS THE **FIVE INVERSIONS.** A TERRORIST CELL BENT ON THE DESTRUCTION OF THE GUARDIANS OF THE UNIVERSE.

CHIEF AMONG THEM, **ATROCITUS.**

ALONG WITH QULL, THEY SOUGHT THE **INNER POWERS** OF THE UNIVERSE. WITH THEIR RITUALS AND SACRIFICES, THEY PEERED INTO THE DEEPEST **DEPTHS** OF THE FUTURE.

AND THEY SAW **DARKNESS.**

A **BLACK** SO **DEVOID** OF LIFE, EVEN THE GUARDIANS' **LIGHT** COULD NOT PENETRATE IT.

THEY SEEK TO TAKE THIS **DARKNESS** FOR THEMSELVES AND TURN IT AGAINST US.

IT WAS FORETOLD, THAT POWER WOULD BE FOUND ON EARTH.

I KNOW YOU DO NOT BELIEVE THESE PROPHECIES, SINESTRO, NOR DO THE GUARDIANS. BUT I ASK, IN THE NAME OF OUR FRIENDSHIP, **TRUST ME.**

YOU MUST STOP THEM FROM UNLEASHING THIS DARKNESS.

IT WILL **DESTROY** THE UNIVERSE.

HE LOOKED... **SCARED**--

WHAT?

WHEN YOU SPOKE TO ABIN SUR, DID YOU SEE ANOTHER BODY?

ANOTHER **BODY,** JORDAN?

ABIN SUR WAS THE ONLY ONE I SAW IN THE SHIP. BUT HE WAS TORE UP PRETTY BAD. I THOUGHT IT WAS FROM THE CRASH. I DIDN'T THINK IT WAS BY **SOMEBODY.**

IT **WAS.**

ATROCITUS **SURVIVED.**

"WE NEED TO *FIND* HIM."

KRIK

KRIK KRIK KRIK
KRIK KRIK KRIK

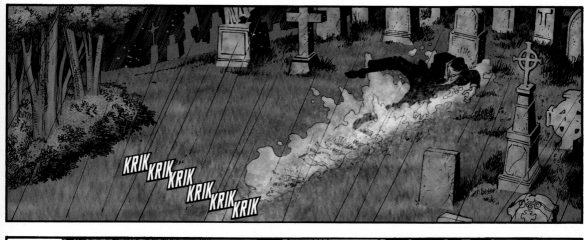

WILLIAM HAND.

KRIK KRIK
KRIK KRIK
KRIK KRIK

YOUR INSIDES HOLD THE DOORWAY TO ABSOLUTE DARKNESS.

ATROCITUS!

FEEL MY **RAGE.**

KID! GET OUT OF HERE!

RUN, DAMMIT!

NNG*GFF!*

WARNING. POWER LEVELS DEPLETING.

POWER LEVELS AT 38.7%

SINESTRO? WHAT'S... HAPPENING?

HE'S BUILT A COSMIC **DIVINING ROD.**

IT CAN **LOCATE** POWER--

--AND IT CAN **TAKE** IT.

WARNING. POWER LEVELS APPROACHING 0.0%

GET ON YOUR **FEET,** JORDAN.

O ONE ELSE HAD TO WATCH THEIR FATHER DIE IN FRONT OF THEIR EYES.

THAT'S WHAT I THOUGHT MOST OF MY LIFE.

I THOUGHT I WAS ALONE.

GROWING UP, THE PILOTS WHO KNEW DAD WOULD LOOK AT ME WITH PITY WHEN I'D BEG TO GO ON A FLIGHT.

THEY ALWAYS REFUSED.

WHEN I FLEW MYSELF, THEY WOULD LOOK AT ME WITH ANNOYANCE. THINKING I WAS BREAKING THE RULES AND PUSHING THE BOUNDARIES UNTIL THE RIVETS POPPED OFF MY WINGS OUT OF ARROGANCE.

NO ONE EVER LOOKED AT ME WITH ANY KIND OF UNDERSTANDING.

NO ONE KNEW WHY I WAS THE WAY I WAS. NOT UNTIL I MET SINESTRO.

JORDAN, FALL BACK.

I'VE NEVER RUN FROM A FIGHT BEFORE, SINESTRO. NOT GONNA START NOW.

YOUR RING IS EMPTY, LANTERN.

YOU ARE NOTHING TO ME.

SSLLAASSHH

GIVE ME YOUR BEST--

GET DOWN

BOOOM

IDIOT!

SSLAATTT

KRIK KRIK KRIK KRIK

YOU ARE STILL HERE, BOY.

DOORWAY TO THE *BLACK*.

WILLIAM HAND...

...YOUR INSIDES HOLD THE POWER THAT WILL *DESTROY* THE GUARDIANS OF THE UNIVERSE.

YOU ARE THE INCUBATOR OF *DEATH* TO ALL!

"FALLING BACK" IS A *MILITARY TACTIC*, JORDAN.

IT IS *NOT* A SIGN OF *FEAR.*

STANDING IN THE *LINE OF FIRE* WITH A *DRAINED* POWER RING, HOWEVER, IS A SIGN OF *STUPIDITY.*

YOU SHOULD BE *DEAD.*

YOU'RE NOT THE *FIRST* ONE TO TELL ME THAT.

I'M *SHOCKED.*

THAT DEVICE ATROCITUS IS HOLDING IS CAPABLE OF *REMOVING* AND *CONTAINING* THE ENERGY WITHIN OUR RINGS.

WE NEED TO KEEP *CLEAR* OF IT AND WE NEED TO *RECHARGE.*

WHAT ARE YOU DOING?

RECALLING *MY POWER BATTERY.*

DON'T TELL ME SALAAK DIDN'T *EDUCATE* YOU ON CONFINED POCKET DIMENSIONS AND THE STORAGE OF PERSONAL CHARGING UNITS.

I KEEP MINE IN MY *LOCKER.*

YOU'VE REDEFINED THE WORD *CARELESS* FOR ME, JORDAN.

SO *I* TAUGHT *YOU* SOMETHING?

JUST *LIGHT UP,* ROOKIE.

OUR PROPHECIES SAY YOU ARE THE *GREATEST* OF THEM ALL.

THEY SAY IF *ANYONE* IS TO OPPOSE OUR *REVENGE*, IT IS *YOU.*

NN...

BUT THEY ALSO SAY YOU HAVE A *WEAKNESS.*

LIKE *ALL* OF THE GUARDIANS' TERRORISTS.

I WILL BATHE IN YOUR BLOOD, *"GREAT ONE."*

NO!

YELLOW...?

...THAT WAS... NOT POSSIBLE...

YOU KNOW MY NAME, ATROCITUS?

GOOD.

TELL THE OTHER *FOUR* OF THE *INVERSIONS* WHO THEY HAVE TO *FEAR*.

GHOOOMMM

SINESTRO. THE *GREATEST* GREEN LANTERN OF THEM ALL.

HEY!

HEY, KID! YOU ALL RIGHT?

HEY--!

LET THE BOY GO, JORDAN.

WHAT DID ATROCITUS WANT WITH HIM?

THEY GAIN POWER THROUGH THE BLOOD OF OTHERS THEY DEEM "DOORWAYS." BEINGS THEY BELIEVE ARE TIED TO THE GREATER FABRIC OF UNIVERSAL POWER.

UTTER NONSENSE.

YOU SAW WHAT I DID, DIDN'T YOU?

WHAT DID YOU DO?

I USED THE RING AGAINST YELLOW.

YOU ASSISTED IN THIS TAKEDOWN AND ARREST, JORDAN, WITHOUT YOUR RING SEEKING A REPLACEMENT.

YOU SURVIVED. THAT'S ENOUGH.

YOU DON'T BELIEVE ME?

YOU DON'T THINK I'VE TRIED TO PIERCE THE SPECTRUM BARRIER? IT IS *FUTILE*. EVEN FOR *ME*.

I *DID*.

ENOUGH.

#$%& YOU.

UNABLE TO TRANSLATE.

HFFF. YOU HAVE TO STAND OUT, DON'T YOU?

YOU CAN'T STAND TO BE UPSTAGED?

BEING A MEMBER OF THE CORPS, YOU'LL NEED TO GET *USED* TO IT.

WHAT MAKES ANYONE THINK I *WANT* TO BE AFTER ALL THIS?

YOU NEED TO GET HOLD OF YOUR *ANGER*, JORDAN. THAT'S WHAT ALMOST GOT YOU *KILLED* TODAY.

I DON'T KNOW *WHAT* OR *WHO* YOU'RE SO *ANGRY* WITH, BUT YOU CONTINUE TO DIRECT IT AT *ME*.

YOU NEED TO *GROW UP*, *DEAL* WITH IT AND GET *ON* WITH YOUR *LIFE*.

YOU KNOW WHAT? I WILL.

RING. TAKE ME TO *CARL FERRIS*.

JORDAN? JORDAN?!

WE HAVE **PROTOCOLS** TO FOLLOW!

I DIDN'T LIKE SINESTRO. BUT HE WAS RIGHT. ALL THAT ANGER WASN'T ABOUT HIM.

I THOUGHT IT'D TAKE ME TO A BEACH HOUSE IN FLORIDA...

...INSTEAD I FOUND MYSELF FLYING DOWN TO HIS HOUSE OUTSIDE COAST CITY.

BLMMBLMM BLMM

BLMMBLMM BLMM

JORDAN?

WHAT...

...WHAT IS THIS?

HE'S SICK.

YOUR FATHER WAS HIS **BEST FRIEND.** AND AFTER THE CRASH...

...IT **TORE** HIM UP INSIDE. AND OVER THE YEARS, THE **GUILT** TOOK ITS TOLL.

HE WAS NEVER GOLFING ON PEBBLE BEACH?

HE'S NEVER PLAYED GOLF IN HIS LIFE. LAST YEAR, WHEN HE GOT TOO SICK TO GET OUT OF BED, FERRIS AIR WAS ALREADY IN TROUBLE.

SO YOU STOPPED FLYING? YOU STARTED RUNNING FERRIS? AND YOU LET EVERYONE THINK YOUR FATHER WAS DOING IT ALL THROUGH **YOU?**

I DIDN'T KNOW WHAT ELSE TO DO.

THAT COMPANY. AFTER MOM AND YOUR FATHER, IT'S ALL **HE** HAD **LEFT.**

HE STILL HAS **YOU.**

I WAS A **SPOILED BRAT.**

WHEN MOM DIED, HE'D GIVE ME ANYTHING I WANTED AS LONG AS I SCREAMED **LOUD** ENOUGH.

ONE DAY, HE **REFUSED.** I DON'T EVEN KNOW WHAT I WAS AFTER, BUT I REMEMBER I SAID...

...I SAID I WISHED **MOM** WAS THERE INSTEAD OF **HIM.**

HE SAW YOU BRING YOUR DAD A BROWN BAG LUNCH AND HE TOLD ME...

...HE WISHED HE HAD A SON LIKE **YOU.**

HE WOULDN'T IF HE **KNEW** ME.

YOU'RE **HERE** FOR HIM. **ME?**

I'VE **NEVER** BEEN THERE FOR **ANYONE** IN MY FAMILY.

ALL THESE YEARS. ALL THIS *TIME.* AND I'VE *WASTED* IT.

I'VE WASTED IT *HATING* SOMEONE. BEING *ANGRY* AT SOMEONE.

SOMEONE WHO *DIDN'T* DESERVE IT.

A *LOT* OF PEOPLE WHO DIDN'T DESERVE IT.

I'M *SORRY,* CAROL.

I'M *SO* SORRY.

YOU'VE JUST WITNESSED THE *TRUE* POWER OF THE RING.

IT HAS HELPED YOU FIND THE *WILL* TO *LIVE.*

IT IS THE MOST *BASIC* ELEMENT WITHIN ONE'S WILLPOWER.

YOU WERE RIGHT.

I KNOW.

YOU AREN'T RIGHT ABOUT *EVERYTHING.*

BUT THE ANGER... THE ANGER I'VE HELD ONTO SINCE I WAS A *KID*...

...THAT'S BEEN FOR *NOTHING.* THAT HASN'T HELPED ANYONE.

BERATING YOU IS *MY* JOB, NOT *YOURS.*

I MYSELF HAVE SUFFERED LOSS, JORDAN. *GREAT* LOSS.

WITHOUT ABIN THERE TO HELP ME, I DOUBT THIS RING WOULD STILL BE *MINE.*

FOR BEINGS LIKE US, OVERCOMING FEAR IS WHAT WE DO BEST. BUT WHEN IT COMES TO GUILT, REGRET... *LOSS...*

...EVEN *GREEN LANTERNS* STRUGGLE WITH THOSE.

NEVER *FORGET* THAT, JORDAN. ONE DAY YOU MAY NEED TO PASS THAT ON TO A ROOKIE AS I HAVE. AS ABIN *DID.*

SO YOU THINK I'LL MAKE IT AS LANTERN NOW?

YOU WILL, IF YOU COME TO UNDERSTAND THE *HONOR* THAT YOU'VE BEEN BESTOWED WITH. IF YOU LEARN THE TRUE *MEANING* BEHIND THE OATH WE RECITE.

AND IF YOU SPEND SOME TIME *OFF* THIS BALL OF MUD AND PRIMITIVE CULTURES AND EXPERIENCE THE WONDER OF THE OTHERS IN YOUR SECTOR.

PERHAPS EVEN IN *MINE.*

THANKS.

YOU ARE WELCOME--

--GREEN LANTERN.

TIME ALLOTMENT EXCEEDED. ILLEGAL FRATERNIZING BETWEEN OFFICERS REGISTERED.

WHAT?

LANTERN 1417.

LANTERN 2814.

YOU HAVE DISOBEYED OUR TERRITORIAL EDICT. YOU WILL REPORT TO OA--

--FOR IMMEDIATE DISCIPLINE.

YOU ARE WELL AWARE OF THE *LIMITS* WE HAVE PUT ON THE CONGREGATION OF OUR OFFICERS *OFF* THE PLANET OA.

THESE ARE THE GUARDIANS OF THE *UNIVERSE?* THEY'RE SO *SMALL--*

SHUT UP.

THIS IS THE *SECOND TIME* YOU HAVE *DISOBEYED* US. AND *AGAIN* WITH THE GREEN LANTERN OF SECTOR 2814.

ALBEIT IT A *DIFFERENT* ONE. THIS IS NOT ABIN SUR.

MY NAME'S *HAL JORDAN.*

THEY *KNOW* THAT.

SINESTRO--?

EXPLAIN YOURSELF.

I WAS SIMPLY ASSISTING THIS OFFICER IN *LOCATING* AND *ARRESTING* THE *KILLER* WHO ENDED THE LIFE OF ABIN SUR.

ATROCITUS OF THE FIVE INVERSIONS.

AND BEFORE YOU SO *ARROGANTLY* RIPPED ME AWAY FROM THAT BACKWARDS BALL OF *DIRT*, I HAD HIM IN *CUSTODY*.

WE ARE WELL *AWARE*.

ATROCITUS WAS *TETHERED* TO YOUR RING.

THIS *TERRORIST* WILL BE RETURNED TO YSMAULT WHERE HE WILL CONTINUE HIS *SENTENCE*--

--AN *ETERNITY* OF IMPRISONMENT.

HOWEVER, THIS ARREST DOES NOT *EXCUSE YOU* FROM BREAKING OUR TERRITORIAL EDICT, SINESTRO.

GREEN LANTERNS MUST ONLY OPERATE IN THEIR *RESPECTIVE* SECTORS. THEY MUST PATROL *INDEPENDENTLY*. THEY MUST *FLY* ON THEIR OWN--

WHY?

WORKING INDEPENDENTLY WILL MAKE YOU **STRONGER,** HAL JORDAN OF EARTH.

YOU WILL **LEARN** THAT THE ENEMIES OF **ORDER** WILL STOP AT **NOTHING** TO SPREAD **CHAOS.**

DO NOT **QUESTION** THE GUARDIANS.

WHY?

WE HAVE LIVED FOR **BILLIONS** OF YEARS.

WHAT WE DO, WE DO FOR THE **WELL-BEING** OF THE **ENTIRE** UNIVERSE.

LIKE THE **MANHUNTERS?**

JORDAN--

THE ANDROIDS THAT DID OUR JOB BEFORE THEY WENT "GLITCHY" AND SLAUGHTERED **EVERY** LIVING BEING IN SECTOR 666 BUT THE FIVE INVERSIONS--?

THEY ARE **LIES** FROM ATROCITUS--

IT **WASN'T** ATROCITUS THAT TOLD US ABOUT THE **MASSACRE.** IT WAS **ABIN SUR.** A MESSAGE--

MORE FABLES TO INSTILL **FEAR** AMONG YOU.

INSTILL FEAR IN **US?** YOU KNOW WHAT **I** THINK?

I THINK **YOU'RE** AFRAID.

YOU *DARE* ACCUSE THE GUARDIANS OF FEELING *FEAR*?

JORDAN. DON'T PUSH IT *TOO* FAR--

I'VE SEEN *WORSE* LIGHT SHOWS, SINESTRO. I'M *NOT* AFRAID OF *THEM.*

BUT I THINK IT'S PRETTY *OBVIOUS...*

...THAT *THEY'RE* AFRAID OF *US.*

THAT'S *ABSURD.*

OUR RINGS DON'T WORK ON *YELLOW,* BUT NO ONE CAN EXPLAIN *WHY.*

"AND THE *BUILDINGS* ON OA, THE CITADEL OF THE GUARDIANS, THEY ALL JUST *HAPPEN* TO BE *YELLOW?*"

"BECAUSE THEY'RE *AFRAID* WE'LL TURN ON THEM LIKE THEIR *ROBOTS* DID."

THEY EXPECT *US* TO OVERCOME OUR FEARS.

WHAT ABOUT WHAT THE GUARDIANS *FEAR?*

AND THAT *TERRITORIAL EDICT?*

THAT EDICT IS $#%?!$%#.

UNABLE TO TRANSLATE.

ENOUGH. YOUR ACCUSATIONS AND DISRESPECT CAUSE US *GREAT* CONCERN.

YOU ARE ON THE VERGE OF *EXPULSION*, HAL JORDAN OF EARTH.

GUARDIANS. YOU EXPEL JORDAN, YOU CAN HAVE *MY* RING AS WELL.

OA *HELP* ME, THE EARTHMAN IS *RIGHT*.

I AM?

QUIET. *PLEASE.*

WE *CAN* BE STRONGER *TOGETHER.*

THE CORPS *SHOULD* WORK IN UNISON WHEN NECESSARY.

AND IT SHOULD BE UP TO *US* TO NOT ONLY HELP OUR FELLOW OFFICERS *GROW*, BUT TO KEEP THEM IN *CHECK.* TO INSURE THAT THE TRAGEDY THAT HAPPENED IN SECTOR 666 *NEVER* HAPPENS AGAIN.

ALL OF *THIS.* THIS STARTED BECAUSE ONE OF YOU *SENT* ME TO ASSIST ABIN SUR'S REPLACEMENT.

ONE OF US?

THE ONE WHO CALLS HIMSELF *"GANTHET."*

"GANTHET"?

WE TAKE NO NAMES.

ONE OF YOU HAS.

WHICH ONE?

I BELIEVE WE HAVE HEARD MUCH TO CONSIDER, SINESTRO. FOR NOW, WE LEAVE THE EARTHMAN WITH HIS RING.

AND OBVIOUSLY, YOU WITH YOURS.

YES. BUT HE IS NOW AS MUCH YOUR RESPONSIBILITY AS KORUGAR AND THE REST OF SECTOR 1417.

WE TRUST THAT IS ACCEPTABLE, SINESTRO...

...GREATEST OF THE GREEN LANTERNS.

Hr.

YES.

"THAT IS ACCEPTABLE."

HNNN!!

FSSSSSSS

I *DID* DO IT.

YOU *DIDN'T* DO IT.

I *DID.*

NO ONE CAN BREAK THROUGH YELLOW, JORDAN. NOT EVEN SINESTRO.

I CAN--

YOU ONLY TRIED LIKE *TWENTY* TIMES, HUMAN! YOU CAN TRY ANOTHER *THOUSAND* AND IT WON'T MAKE A DIFFERENCE.

I BELIEVE HIM.

YOU, TOMAR-RE? YOU ALWAYS HAD FAITH *FAR* TOO READILY.

I SUPPOSE THAT IS ONE THING ABIN TAUGHT ME THAT HE NEVER TAUGHT YOU.

I SUPPOSE...

...I MUST *GO.*

I DO NOT HAVE TIME FOR ANY MORE *GAMES...*

...THE GUARDIANS HAVE BOTHERED ME WITH THE *TASK* OF RETURNING ATROCITUS TO YSMAULT.

SINESTRO.

IF YOU'RE GOING TO SAY ANYTHING, JORDAN, SAY "I WON'T MAKE YOU *REGRET* THIS."

I WON'T.

THAT IS ALL I NEED TO HEAR, BECAUSE, *UNFORTUNATELY*, A "GOODBYE" IS NOT APPROPRIATE.

WE WILL RECONVENE IN ONE MONTH SO THAT I MAY EVALUATE YOUR PROGRESS.

BUT *NEXT* TIME--

--YOU'RE COMING TO *MY* WORLD.

"FERRIS IS LETTING *YOU* FLY?"

"IT'S NOT LIKE SHE HAD MUCH OF A CHOICE, TOM."

I GUESS NOT.

BUT BEING THE ONLY PILOT--

FOR NOW.

BEING THE ONLY PILOT, YOU'RE GOING TO BE LOGGING A HELLUVA LOT OF *FLIGHT TIME.*

THAT'S WHAT I'M HOPING.

I STILL DON'T GET WHY YOU WANT TO FLY A *PLANE* WHEN YOU'VE GOT THAT *MAGIC RING.*

THE RING'S NOT *MAGIC.* THE PLANES ARE.

SPEAKING OF. WHICH ONE AM I TAKING UP TODAY?

THAT ONE OVER THERE.

FWUMP

THIS IS...THIS IS THAT HUNK OF JUNK. THIS IS THE PLANE MY DAD FLEW ME IN. BUT--

I'M GOOD, *huh?* ONLY TOOK ME THREE WEEKS.

IT'S AMAZING, TOM.

IT SEEMED LIKE SHE MEANT A LOT TO YOU. I TOLD MISS FERRIS. SHE SAID I COULD FIX IT UP.

CAROL DID?

WHEN EVERY OTHER PILOT *LEFT*, I NEEDED *SOMETHING* TO KEEP YOU HERE.

EDWARDS AIR FORCE BASE. HANGAR 44.

ANYTHING SPECIAL PLANNED TONIGHT?

HEADING DOWN TO PANCHO'S WITH THE GUYS. MY GIRLFRIEND'S BEEN A PAIN LATELY. SHE'S BEEN ON MY CASE ABOUT THE "NEXT LEVEL" OF OUR RELATIONSHIP.

I TOLD HER THE NEXT LEVEL IS ME MOVIN' ON OUT!

I HAVE A GIRLFRIEND TOO.

DO YOU HEAR ME?

HELLO?

ANYONE? DO YOU HEAR ME?

YOU CAN'T LEAVE ME IN HERE. THIS IS A TERRIBLY EMPTY PLACE! A VILE PLACE!

I'M NOT LIKE THAT ALIEN SHIP! I'M NOT HERE TO BE POKED AND PRODDED!

DON'T LISTEN TO THE GREEN LANTERN!

HE IS AMAZING THOUGH. THE LIFE HE LIVES IS SO THRILLING.

THE LEAPS AND THE FLIGHTS AND THE WOMEN.

THE WOMEN.

I WANT TO BE A PART OF THAT EXCITEMENT. OH, IT'LL BE WONDERFUL WHEN I AM AGAIN!

YES, OH, YES!

I'M FEELING BETTER ALREADY.

...REPORTS OF MORE **STRANGE LIGHTS** IN THE SKY ARE POURING IN.

COAST CITY HOSPITAL
CCH

U.F.O.'S? SECRET AIR FORCE TEST FLIGHTS? OR ARE THESE RUMORS OF A GLOWING GREEN **MAN** TRUE?

IS THE **GREEN LANTERN** REAL?

WITH THE RECENT APPEARANCE OF **SUPERMAN** IN METROPOLIS, COULD COAST CITY HAVE ITS VERY OWN PROTECTOR? AN EMERALD WARRIOR--?

KLANK

KLK

CHRIST.

I D-D-DIDN'T DO ANYTHING **WRONG.**

STAND **UP.** STAND UP AND GET AWAY FROM THAT--

FWATEE!

FWASSSH

IT'S OKAY. DEAD IS G-G-GOOD.

DEAD IS **GOOD.**

YOUR HOMEWORLD WILL SOON DESCEND INTO CIVIL *UNREST*. *VIOLENT* RIOTS. A *BLOODY* COUP.

YOUR PEOPLE WILL PLUNGE INTO *MADNESS* AS YOU SAVE WORLDS *NOT* YOUR OWN.

CHAOS WILL SPIN IT OUT OF YOUR *CONTROL*.

YOU THINK ME A *FOOL*, ATROCITUS?

KORUGAR WILL *NEVER* EMBRACE *CHAOS*. NOT AS LONG AS I AM AROUND TO INSTILL *ORDER*.

I FEEL *NO* FEAR, DEMONS.

NO FEAR OF *ANY* KIND.

THEN ONE DAY, YOU WILL FEEL MY *RAGE*, GREEN LANTERN.

AND YOU WILL *BURN* BY IT.

HAL?

JIM?

JACK'S NOT COMING.

I'M SORRY.

I DIDN'T THINK HE WOULD.

I DON'T *BLAME* HIM. I WOULDN'T HAVE BLAMED YOU *EITHER*.

I'VE *NEVER* BEEN A GOOD *BROTHER*.

THAT'S NOT TRUE, HAL.

IT *IS*, JIM. I'VE NEVER OPENED UP AND TALKED TO YOU. NOT EVEN ABOUT DAD.

I NEVER TRIED TO BE A *PART* OF YOUR *LIFE*.

BUT I *WANT* TO BE A PART OF IT, JIM. I WANT TO BE A *GOOD BROTHER*.

I WANT TO LET YOU IN.

BWOOOSHHH

HAL? HAL, WHAT'S GOING ON?

THE END.

The adventure continues in...

THE WATCHTOWER.

HEAD-QUARTERS OF THE JUSTICE LEAGUE OF AMERICA.

JORDAN?

THE UNIFORM **FITS**.

THE **RING** FITS **BETTER**. ALWAYS DID.

A CIRCLE OF NEVER-ENDING **LIGHT**. SYMBOL OF RENEWED **LIFE**.

IT'S NO **MISTAKE** THEY WERE CHOSEN TO REPRESENT THE **POWER** OF THE **GREEN LANTERN CORPS**.

I TOLD YOU, SINESTRO.

GET THE HELL **AWAY** FROM THEM.

WHEN I WAS FIRST **RECRUITED**, I WAS TOLD--

--"DO NOT CHALLENGE THOSE MORE POWERFUL THAN YOU."

FUNNY STUFF.

THAT FELT
GOOD.

War erupts between the Green Lantern Corps and Sinestro in...

I HAVE BEEN TO EVERY CORNER OF EVERY SECTOR OF THE UNIVERSE, AND I HAVE LEARNED ONE THING.

THE UNIVERSE *NEEDS* TO CHANGE.

WE LIVE IN A PLACE *ROTTING* WITH HEDONISM AND CHAOS. A PLACE UNTAMED AND MORALLY DEVOID. A PLACE OF *DARKNESS*.

WHEN I WAS INDUCTED INTO THE GREEN LANTERN CORPS, I BELIEVED I HAD FINALLY *ESCAPED* THE DARKNESS. I WORKED HARD TO VALIDATE THE POWER RING'S SELECTION.

I TORE MY HOME PLANET OF KORUGAR *FREE* FROM SIN.

I BROUGHT ORDER AND VOWED TO DO THE SAME FOR THE *REST* OF SECTOR 1417... AND THEN, WITH THE CORPS' SUPPORT, THE REST OF THE UNIVERSE.

FOR A TIME THE GUARDIANS EVEN CALLED ME THE "GREATEST" OF THE GREEN LANTERNS.

UNTIL AN EARTHMAN *I* TRAINED TOOK *EVERYTHING* FROM ME.

HAL JORDAN CALLED ME A *FASCIST* FOR THE ORDER I BESTOWED UPON KORUGAR.

I WAS STRIPPED OF MY RING.

LABELED THE *FIRST* RENEGADE OF THE *GREEN LANTERN CORPS*, I WAS BANISHED TO THE UNDERBELLY OF THE UNIVERSE, THE ANTIMATTER UNIVERSE...

...AND *DELIVERED* BACK INTO *DARKNESS*.

FOR THE FIRST TIME IN MY LIFE--

--I FELT *FEAR*.

AND I WAS *BLINDED* BY ITS BRILLIANCE.

I BELIEVED *FEAR* TO BE PART OF THE CHAOS I ABHOR, BUT IT WAS MORE CONTROLLING THAN ALL THE WILLPOWER IN THE UNIVERSE.

AND IT WOULD BE *MINE*.

RAYNER IS A *FOOL*.

I WILL *SLICE* THE CREATURE'S CHEST *OPEN* AND RIP OUT HIS USELESS *HEART*.

NO.

YOU WILL *RESPECT* HIM.

DAMN RIGHT.

GREEN ARROW SAYS *HI*.

YOU WILL BE *MINE*, ALLEY RAT.

AND THE UNIVERSE...

...THE UNIVERSE *WILL* CHANGE.

THE GREEN LANTERN CORPS WILL CHANGE.

IN *BLACKEST* DAY... IN *BRIGHTEST* NIGHT...

...BEWARE YOUR *FEARS* MADE INTO LIGHT...

...LET THOSE WHO TRY TO *STOP* WHAT'S *RIGHT*...

...*BURN* LIKE MY *POWER*--